W9-AUF-657

2011 GREATEST Pop & MOVIE Hits

Arranged by Carol Matz

THE BIGGEST MOVIES ★ THE GREATEST ARTISTS

CONTENTS

Alfred

Produced by
Alfred Music Publishing Co., Inc.
P.O. Box 10003
Van Nuys, CA 91410-0003
alfred.com

Printed in USA.

ISBN-10: 0-7390-8273-6
ISBN-13: 978-0-7390-8273-7

 Alfred Cares. Contents printed on 100% recycled paper.

BILLIONAIRE

Words and Music by
Peter Hernandez, Philip Lawrence,
Ari Levine and Travis McCoy
Arranged by Carol Matz

Moderate reggae

Chorus:

I wan-na be a bil - lion - aire so freak - in' bad,_____

buy all of the things I nev - er had.

I wan-na be on the cov - er of Forbes mag - a - zine,_____

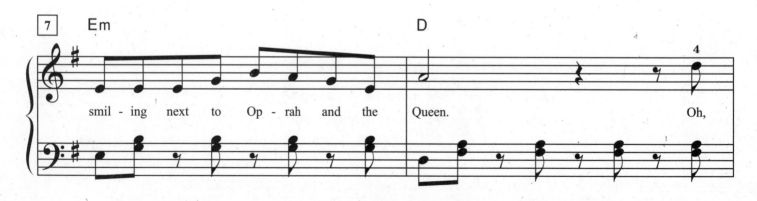

smil - ing next to Op - rah and the Queen. Oh,

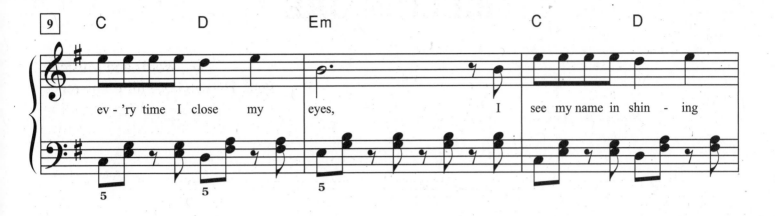

Bridge:

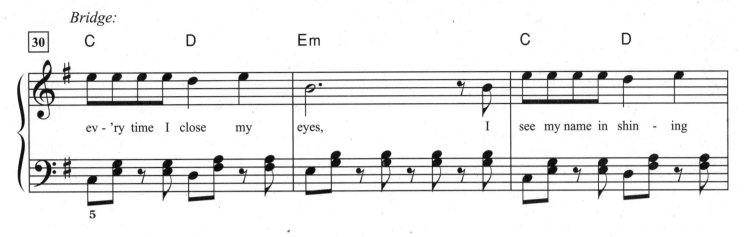

ev - 'ry time I close my eyes, I see my name in shin - ing

lights, a dif-f'rent cit - y ev - 'ry night, oh, I

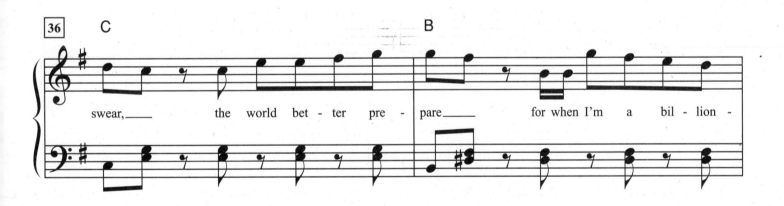

swear, the world bet - ter pre - pare for when I'm a bil - lion -

aire. Oh, oh, when I'm a bil-lion - aire. Oh, oh.

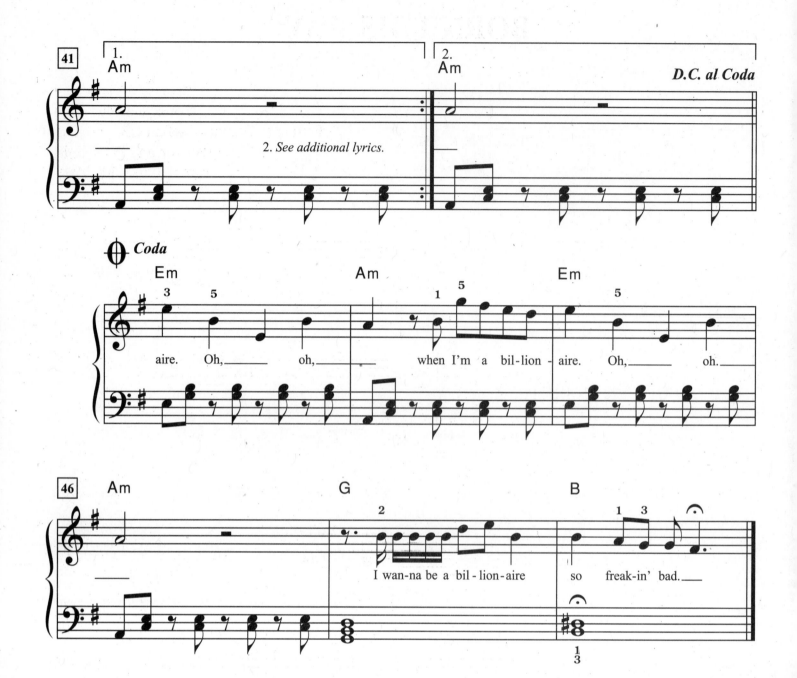

Verse 2:
(Rap)
I'll be playing basketball with the President
Dunking on his delegates,
Then I'll compliment him on his political etiquette,
Toss a couple milli in the air just for the heck of it,
But keep the fives, twenties, tens, and Bens completely separate.
Yeah, I'll be in a whole new tax bracket.
We in a recession, but let me take a crack at it.
I'll probably take whatever's left and just split it up,
So everybody that I love can have a couple bucks.
And not a single tummy around me
Would know what hungry was, eating good, sleeping soundly.
I know we all have a similar dream.
Go in your pocket, pull out your wallet, put it in the air and sing.

BORN THIS WAY

Words and Music by
Fernando Garibay, Stefani Germanotta,
Jeppe Laursen and Paul Blair
Arranged by Carol Matz

Moderately

Verse:

1. My ma-ma told me when I was young, we're all born su-per-stars.
2. *See additional lyrics.*

She rolled my hair and put my lip-stick on

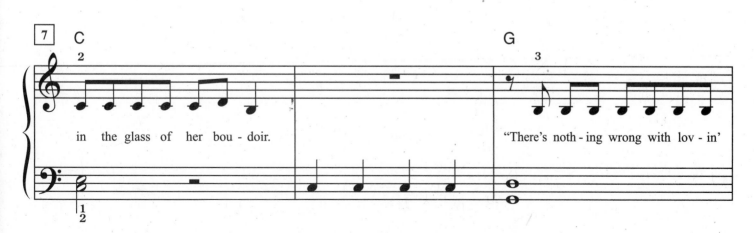

in the glass of her bou-doir. "There's noth-ing wrong with lov-in'

Chorus:

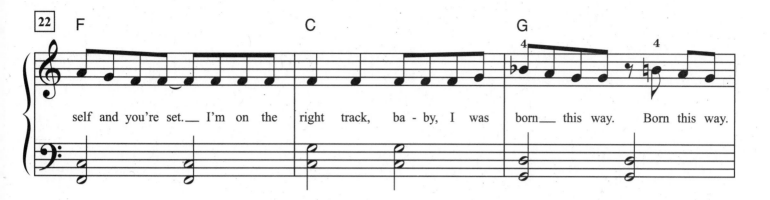

self and you're set.__ I'm on the right track, ba - by, I was born__ this way. Born this way.

There ain't no oth - er way, ba - by, I was born this way. Ba - by, I was born this way.__

__ Born this way. There ain't no oth - er way, ba - by, I was born this way.

Right track, ba - by, I was born__ this way.__ born__ this way. No mat - ter

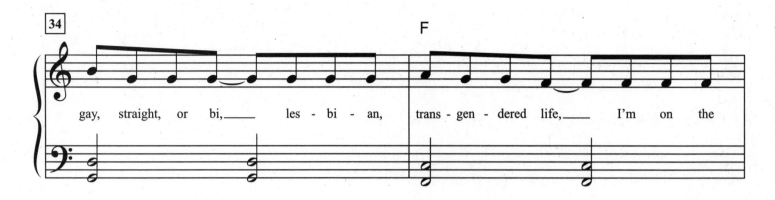

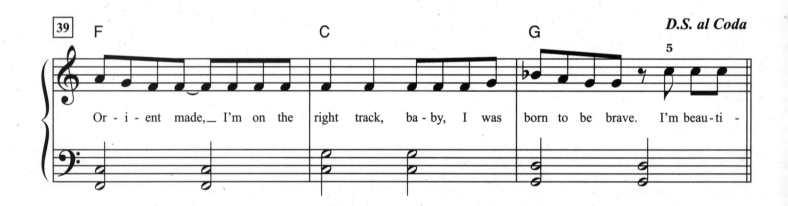

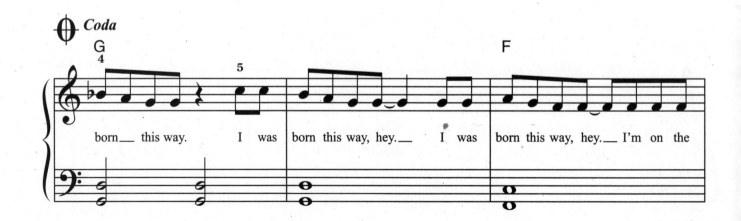

Verse 2:
Give yourself prudence, and love your friends.
Subway kid, rejoice your truth.
In the religion of the insecure,
I must be myself, respect my youth.
A different lover is not a sin.
Believe capital H.I.M.
I love my life, I love this record and,
Mi amore vole fe ya. *(Same DNA.)*
(To Chorus:)

BORN TO BE SOMEBODY

Words and Music by Diane Warren
Arranged by Carol Matz

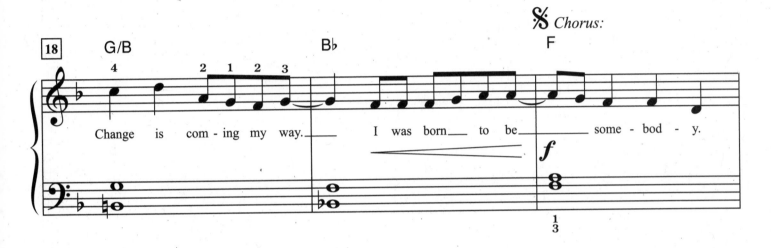

14

15

Verse 2:
This life can kick you around.
This world can make you feel small.
But they will not keep me down.
I was born to stand tall.
I'm going all the way.
I can feel it, I believe it.
I'm here, I'm here to stay.
(To Chorus:)

FIREWORK

Words and Music by
Katy Perry, Mikkel Eriksen, Tor Erik Hermansen,
Sandy Wilhelm and Ester Dean
Arranged by Carol Matz

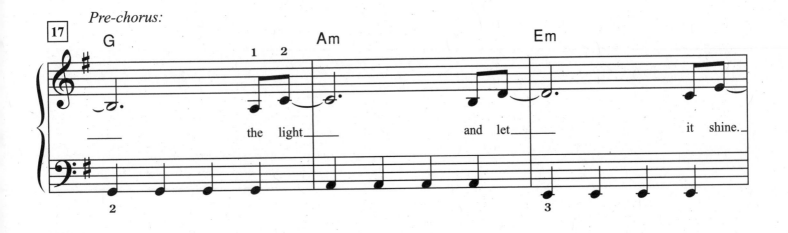

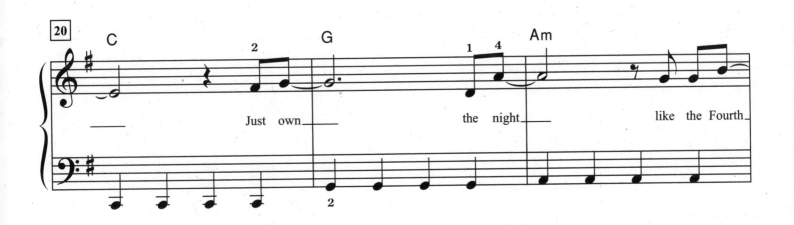

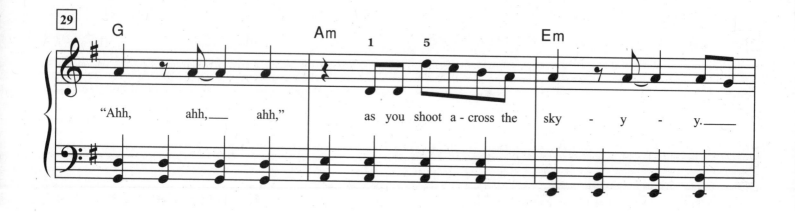

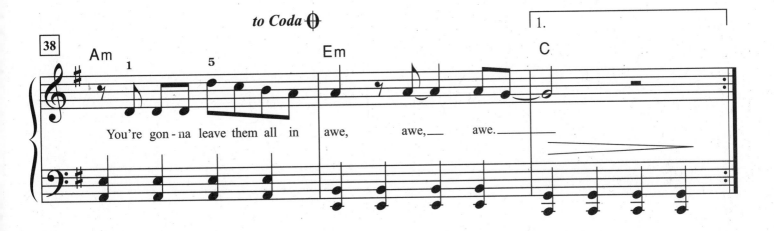

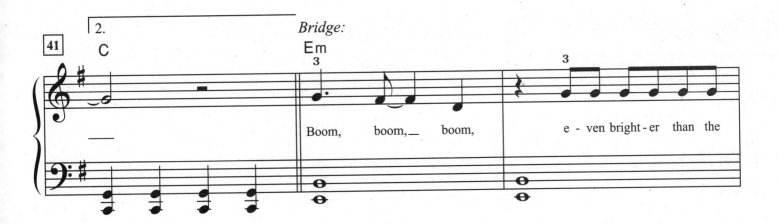

D.S. al Coda

And now, it's time to let it through._____ 'Cause ba - by, you're a

Coda

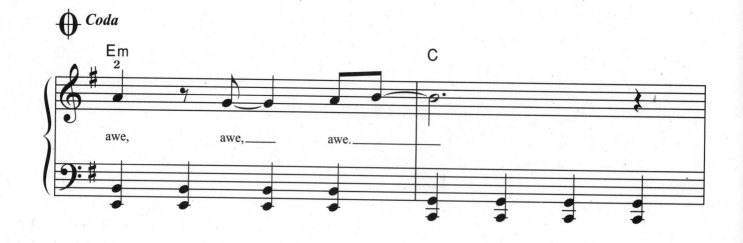

awe, awe,_____ awe._____

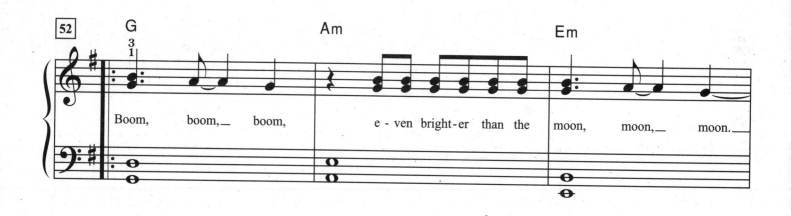

Boom, boom,___ boom, e - ven bright-er than the moon, moon,___ moon._____

FORGET YOU

Words and Music by
Christopher Brown, Peter Hernandez, Ari Levine,
Philip Lawrence and Thomas "Cee Lo" Callaway
Arranged by Carol Matz

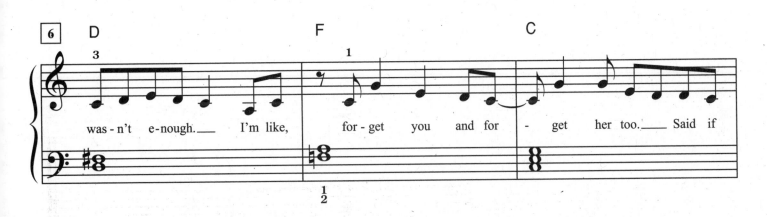

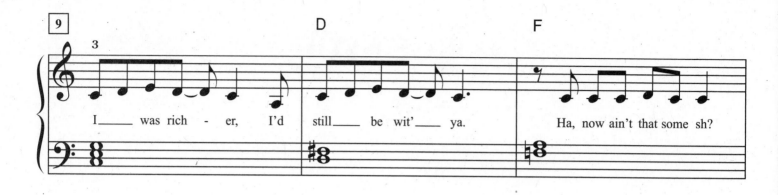

I_____ was rich - er, I'd still_____ be wit'_____ ya. Ha, now ain't that some sh?

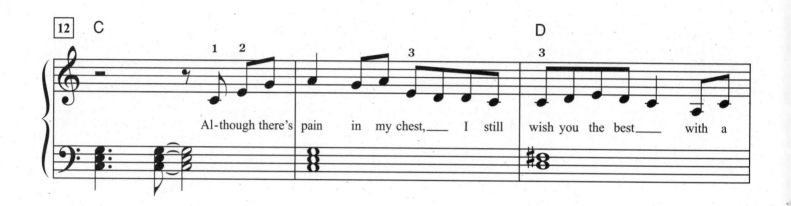

Al-though there's pain in my chest,_____ I still wish you the best_____ with a

to Coda

for - get you._____

1. Yeah, I'm sor - ry can't af-ford a Fer-
2. *See additional lyrics.*

Verse:

ra - ri, but that don't mean I can't get you there._____ I guess he's an

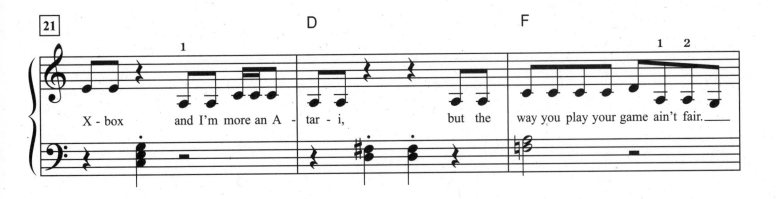

X - box and I'm more an A - tar - i, but the way you play your game ain't fair.____

I pit - y the fool____ that falls in love with you,____ oh, oh.

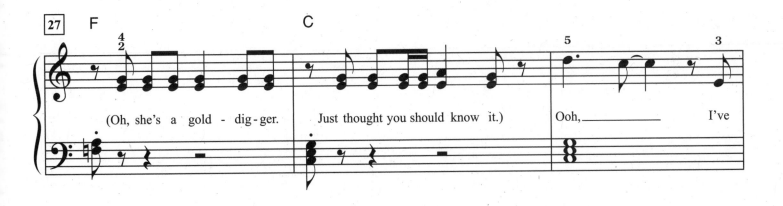

(Oh, she's a gold - dig - ger. Just thought you should know it.) Ooh,____ I've

got some news for you,____ ha ha. See you

24

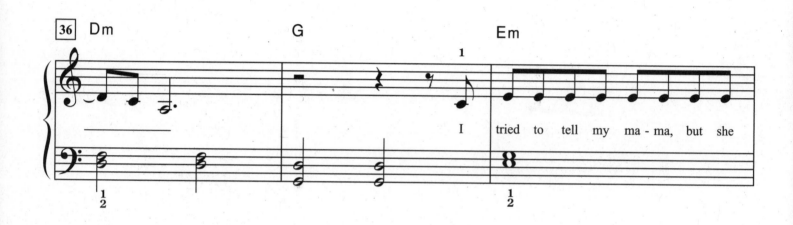

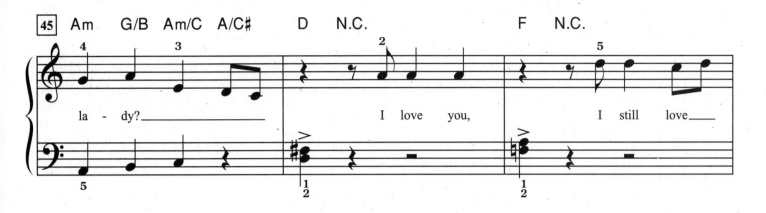

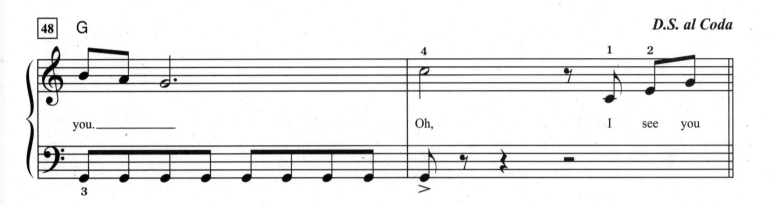

Verse 2:
Now, I know that I had to borrow,
Beg and steal and lie and cheat,
Tryin' to keep ya, tryin' to please ya,
'Cause being in love with your a** ain't cheap.

GRENADE

Words and Music by
Claude Kelly, Peter Hernandez, Brody Brown,
Philip Lawrence, Ari Levine and Andrew Wyatt
Arranged by Carol Matz

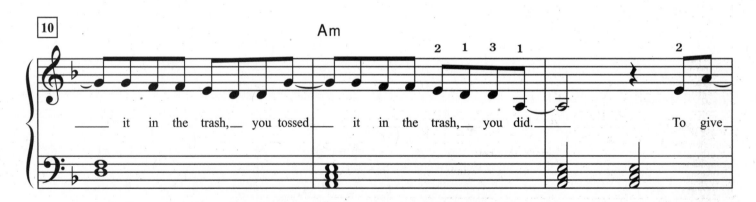

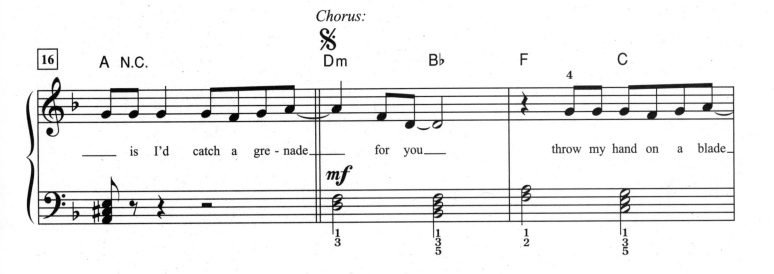

go through all____ this pain,_____ take a bul - let straight through my brain.

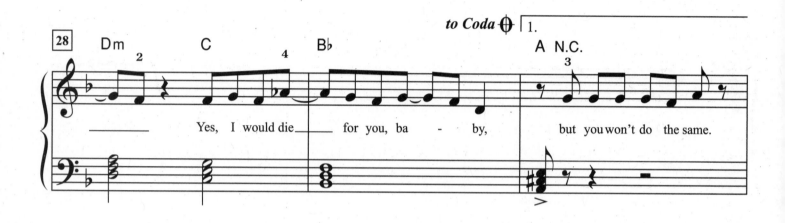

to Coda ⊕

Yes, I would die____ for you, ba - by, but you won't do the same.

but you won't do the same.

Bridge:

If my bod-y was on fi-re, ooh, you'd

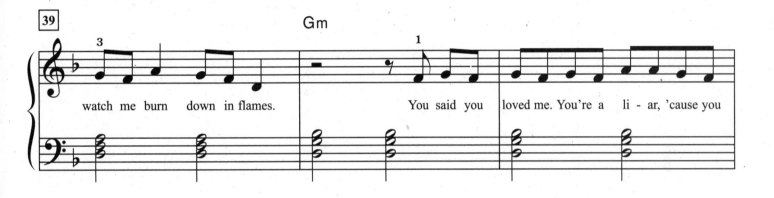

watch me burn down in flames. You said you loved me. You're a li-ar, 'cause you

nev-er, ev-er, ev-er did, ba-by.

D.S. al Coda

But, dar-ling, I'd still catch a gren-ade

30

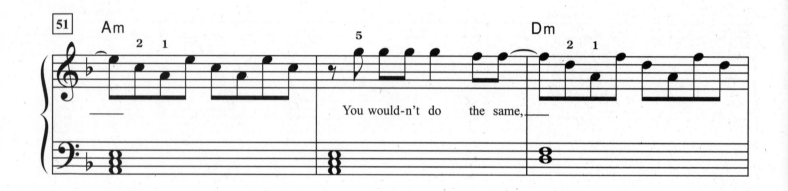

Verse 2:
Black, black, black and blue, beat me 'til I'm numb.
Tell the devil I said "Hey" when you get back to where you're from.
Mad woman, bad woman, that's just what you are.
Yeah, you'll smile in my face then rip the brakes out my car.
Gave you all I had and you tossed it in the trash,
You tossed it in the trash, you did.
To give me all your love is all I ever asked.
'Cause what you don't understand is I'd catch a grenade for you...
(To Chorus:)

HAVEN'T MET YOU YET

Words and Music by
Michael Bublé, Alan Chang and Amy Foster
Arranged by Carol Matz

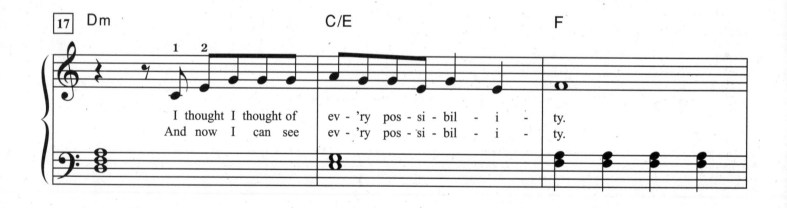

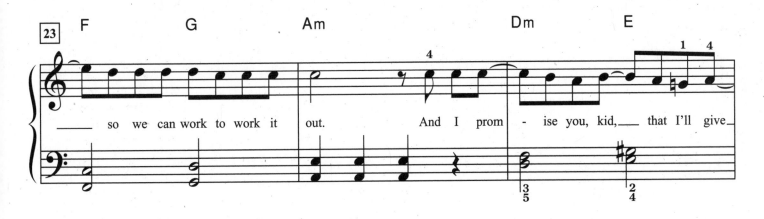

23 F   G   Am   Dm   E

so we can work to work it out.   And I prom - ise you, kid,___ that I'll give___

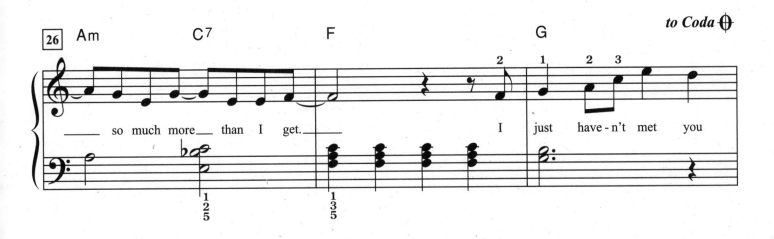

26 Am   C7   F   G   *to Coda*

___ so much more___ than I get.___   I just have - n't met you

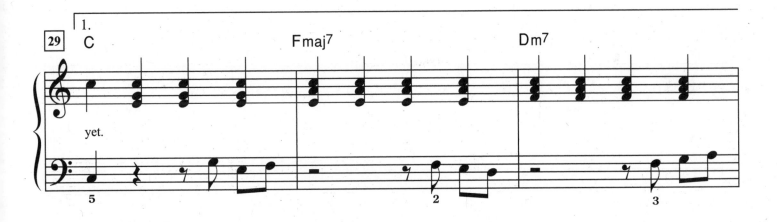

29 1.   C   Fmaj7   Dm7

yet.

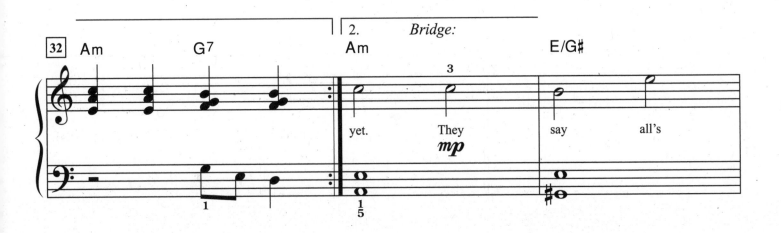

32 Am   G7   2. *Bridge:*   Am   E/G♯

yet.   They   say   all's

mp

34

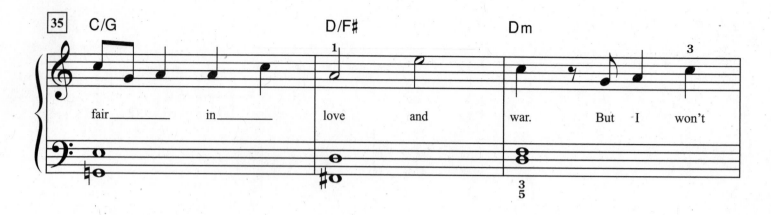

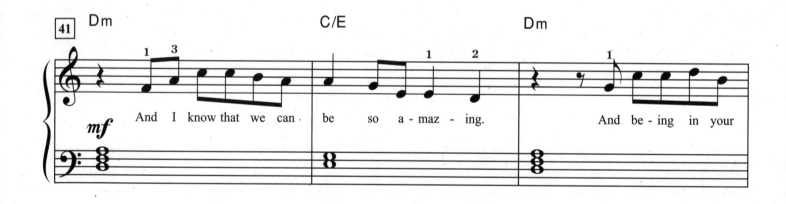

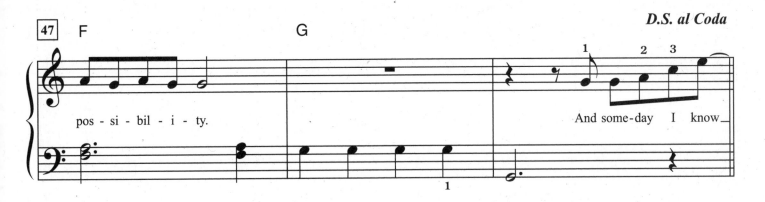

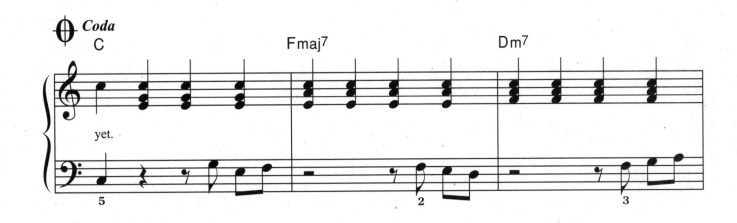

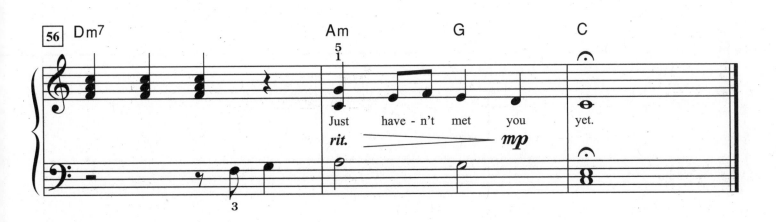

JAR OF HEARTS

Words and Music by
Drew Lawrence, Christina Perri and Barrett Yeretsian
Arranged by Carol Matz

% *Chorus:*

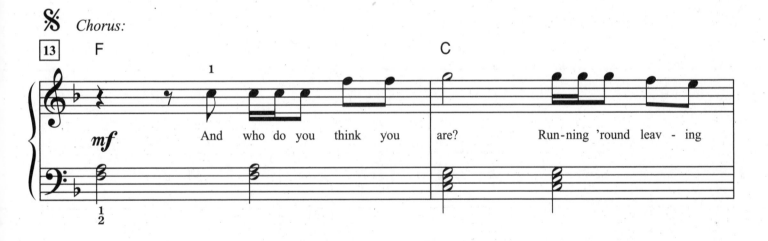

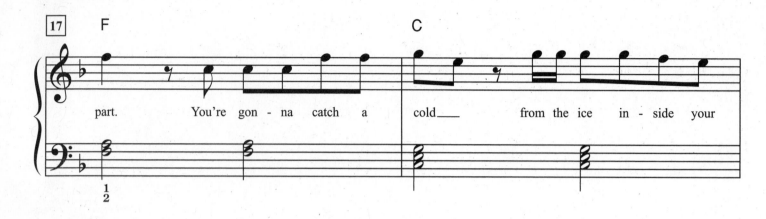

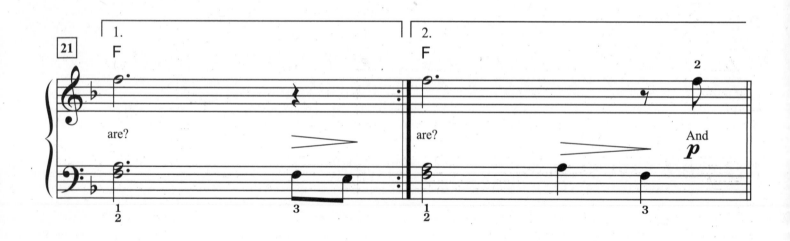

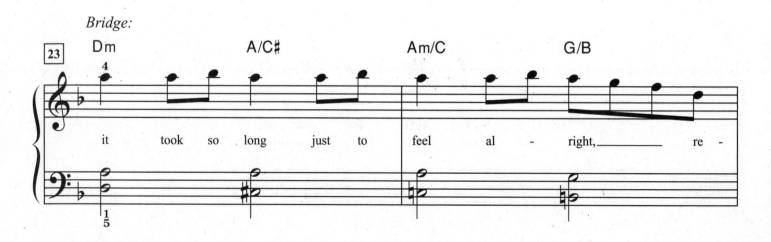

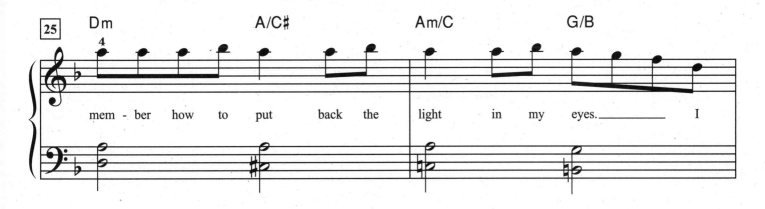

mem - ber how to put back the light in my eyes._____ I

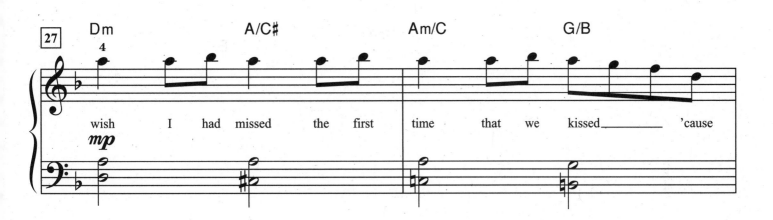

wish I had missed the first time that we kissed_____ 'cause

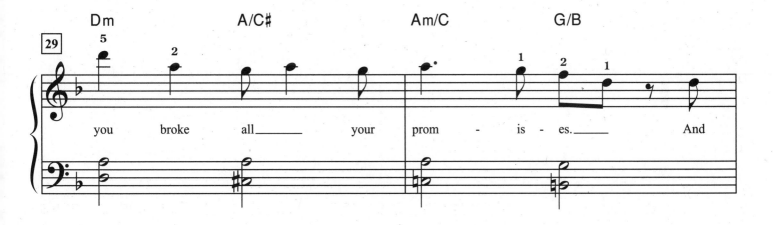

you broke all_____ your prom - is - es._____ And

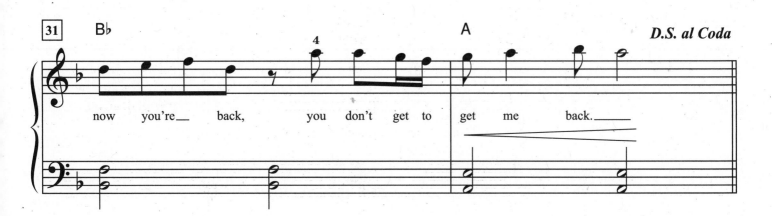

now you're__ back, you don't get to get me back._____

D.S. al Coda

40

Verse 2:
I heard you're asking all around
If I am anywhere to be found.
But I have grown too strong
To ever fall back in your arms.
And I learned to live half alive,
And now you want me one more time.
(To Chorus:)

JUST THE WAY YOU ARE (AMAZING)

Words and Music by
Khalil Walton, Peter Hernandez,
Philip Lawrence, Ari Levine and Khari Cain
Arranged by Carol Matz

think that she don't see what I see. But ev - 'ry time she asks me, "Do I look o - kay?" I

Chorus:

say... When I see your face,

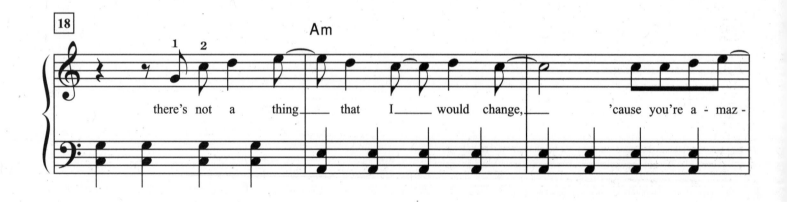

there's not a thing that I would change, 'cause you're a - maz -

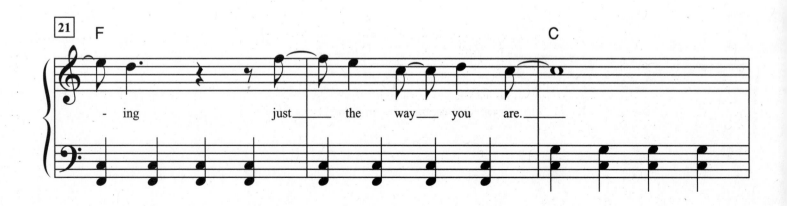

- ing just the way you are.

Verse 2:
Her lips, her lips, I could kiss them all day if she'd let me.
Her laugh, her laugh she hates, but I think it's so sexy.
She's so beautiful and I tell her every day.
Oh, you know, you know, you know I'd never ask you to change.
If perfect's what you're searching for, then just stay the same.
So don't even bother asking if you look okay. You know I'll say...
(To Chorus:)

NOT LIKE THE MOVIES

Words and Music by
Katy Perry and Greg Wells
Arranged by Carol Matz

45

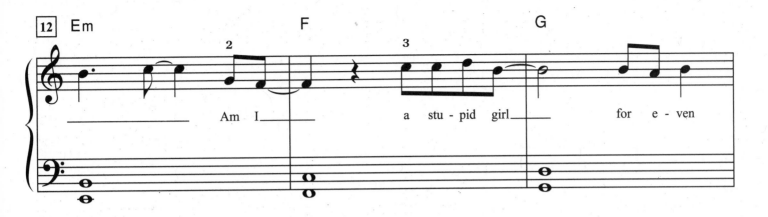

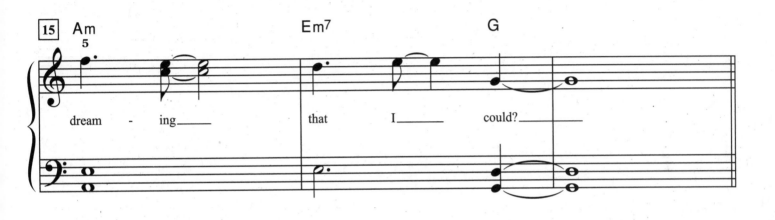

Chorus:

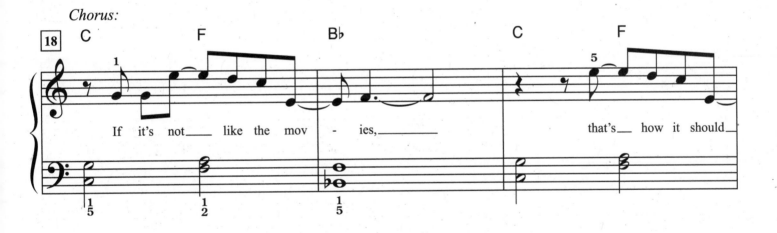

Bridge:

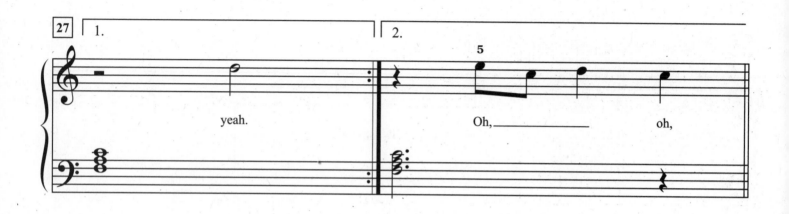

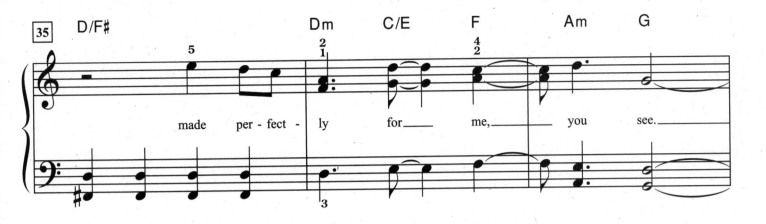

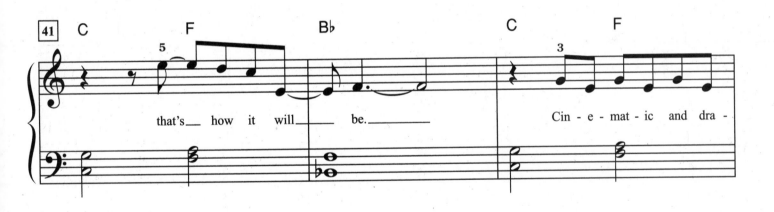

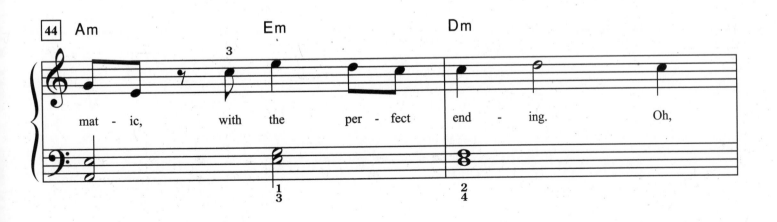

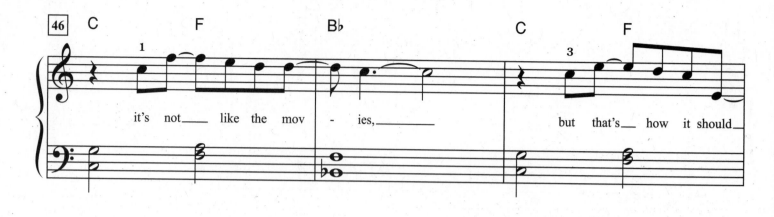

it's not___ like the mov - ies,_____ but that's__ how it should

___ be._____ When he's the one, you'll come un - done, and your world will stop

spin - ing. And it's just the be - gin - ing.

Verse 2:
Snow White said when I was young,
"One day my prince will come."
So I wait for that date.
They say it's hard to meet your match,
Gotta find my better half,
So we make perfect shapes.
If stars don't align, if it doesn't stop time,
If you can't see the sign, wait for it.
One hundred percent, worth every penny spent,
He'll be the one that finishes your sentences.
(To Chorus:)

OBLIVIATE

(from *Harry Potter and The Deathly Hallows, Part 1*)

By Alexandre Desplat
Arranged by Carol Matz

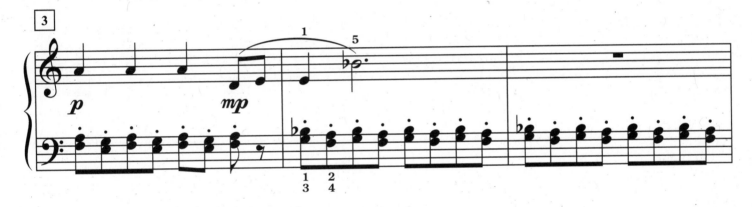

YOU HAVEN'T SEEN THE LAST OF ME

(from *Burlesque*)

Words and Music by Diane Warren
Arranged by Carol Matz

𝄋 *Chorus:*

I've been brought down to my

knees. And I've been pushed way past the

point of break - ing, but I can take it. I'll be

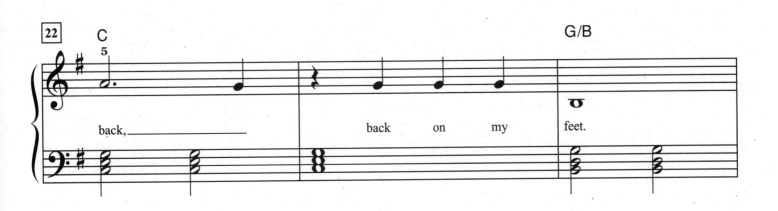

back, back on my feet.

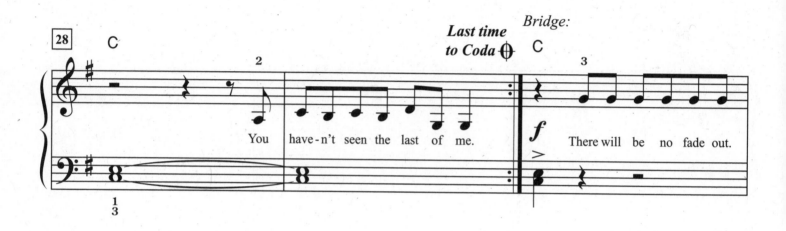

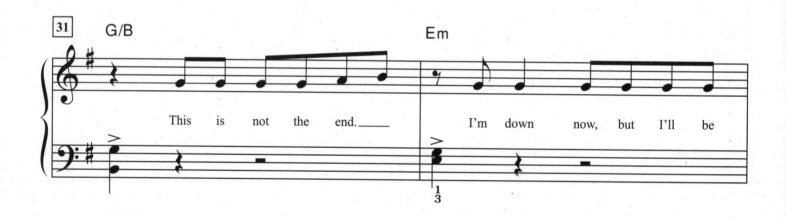

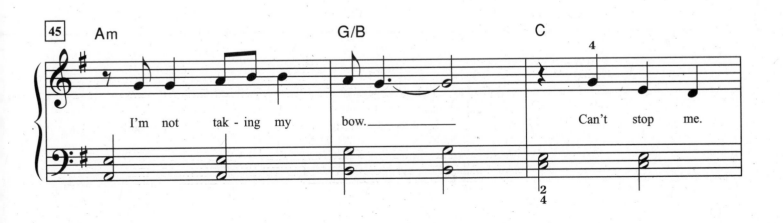

Verse 2:
They can say that I won't stay around,
But I'm gonna stand my ground.
You're not gonna stop me. You don't know me,
You don't know who I am.
Don't count me out so fast.
(To Chorus:)